UNDER THE
SANGRE DE CRISTO

UNDER THE
SANGRE DE CRISTO

by

PAUL HORGAN

**NORTHLAND
PRESS**

This book was previously published
in a signed and numbered letterpress edition
by The Rydal Press, Santa Fe, New Mexico.

ISBN 0-87358-441-4 softcover
ISBN 0-87358-440-6 hardcover
Library of Congress Catalog Card Number 86-46374
Composed and Printed in the United States of America

for
SALLY AND ZIG

CONTENTS

FOREWORD

TWO OF THE MOST STRIKING COMMUNITIES IN THE
United States are Santa Fe and Taos, in New Mexico.

Both lie under the great shadow of the Sangre de Cristo
Range of the southernmost Rocky Mountains and show a
common historical pattern. Their succession of sovereignties
poses the same design—originally that of the Indian, then
the Spanish, then the Mexican, and finally the prevailing
reach of the United States, all traceable from the prehis-
toric age to the present—with visible, and cherished, evi-
dences of each culture under radical change.

The imaginary annals of Santa Fe and Taos, here gathered together for the first time, suggest periods of change
through sketches of persons to be thought of as allegorical
embodiments of their successive epochs—a masque of the
procession that made its way with the coming of the post-
Indian centuries in Santa Fe and Taos. In scheme and
rhetoric the episodes are clothed in a certain formality to
evoke atmospheres of other times.

"From the Royal City" first appeared in *The Yale Review*,
December 1932, and was reprinted in 1936 for Clifford
McCarthy and the Villagra Bookshop by The Rydal Press
at Santa Fe in both cloth and paper covers. "Taos Valley"
first appeared in separate segments—the first four episodes
in *The Yale Review*, September 1944, the fifth in *The Saturday
Review*, May 16, 1942 (which was included later in my short
story collection, *The Peach Stone*). "Taos Valley" appears
here complete for the first time in book form.

Middletown, Connecticut   P.H.

ONE:

FROM THE
ROYAL CITY

I   1690

THE CAPTAIN GENERAL

THE CAPTAIN GENERAL, a huge man made for wearing armor, knew in the year 1690 that what he had to conquer was a thing aside from intelligence. Spain, Europe, all that he knew with his heart and his half-forgotten memory of race and family, were counters in the game of character he played with himself.

It was another matter, taking strange weapons, to cross over mountains in the blue of winter and come down on the tawny plateaus in spring like a vengeance upon Indians.

The Captain General, intelligent with the flowery thoughts of his European time, learned his new land, and marched with an army that was a burlesque of the military in all except heart. He crossed every pueblo in his province, making, in the name of God, the cruciform gesture; and lessening the sincerity of that no whit by resorting to musketry if necessary. It was indubitable that God was on his side; but with the whole country pitted against the new man—with space as great a menace as Apaches, and sudden final spendings of endurance; horses and men willing to die in the yellow hills studded with black bushes of scrub pine—the triumphs of conquest must be, he knew, won severely with defeat and transfiguration of inhabitant and culture.

Such a task took imagination, it took ruthlessness; and there was plenty of both in an educated man of 1690. Authority was sacred. And a man's life was subject to ideals, whose expression must be visible.

The Captain General lived in the Palace of the Governors, with the plaza of the Royal City of the Holy Faith of Saint Francis before its long portal, and a garden in its rear. It was the greatest building in the province, and the Captain General, walking through his dozen rooms, one after another, to reach an audience, felt security and royalty that were explicit. The walls were so thick that the futility of attack was clear, even to the resentful Indians. The low thick ceiling turned away the sun and prevented the snow from chilling the rooms, where fireplaces flashed and danced with fires made from piñon wood, which sent up into the sharp air of the mountains an incense sweeter than the smell of wild flowers.

There were few enough comforts, hardly any time for them; and the Captain General earned his marquisate from Felipe V by putting on his woolen tunic and breeches, strapping his armor against these protective cloths, dropping a serape over the metal to keep it cool from the sun, and leading his men on horseback, with a mule train of supplies, out over the rolling deserts to the belligerent pueblos.

The conflicts that happened, under pink mud walls, represented the forces of the Renaissance against those of the Middle Ages.

The Captain General directed fire from musketry that amazed and slaughtered the Indian, who, hundreds of years more ignorant about Christ and gunpowder, rained arrows

[4]

and stones upon the conquerors, and sheets of boiling water, and cried with desperation upon gods of earth and sky.

One time the Captain General concluded a victory against a wicked tribe; his guns destroyed their hundreds, his soldiers captured women and children, who would become slaves and very valuable. In a gesture of finality the defeated Indian chief hanged himself in the heart of his town.

But in the Royal City, when evening came down from the mountains, where white snow showed always against the darker blue, or darker green, or black, of the sky, the sound of bells ringing to the glory of God assured the Captain General that the proper order was established. He was a good man, simple in his submission of his armed strength to the first tenets of the church. No one could be trusted here, he thought, except his priests, and a few soldiers, his horses, and the image he carried of his own vital necessity.

It is true that intrigues arose against him; and while he waited in the militant pride of his station, for imprisonment, the bitterness that he felt was enriched by memories of the conquests of his arm and will.

How beautiful the valley of the Rio Grande was when he marched up in the springtime! The yellow river went widely down the fertile land, where willows leaned idly over the sandy run, and pale green grass, sharp and tender in early growth, was crushed by the stamp and suck of his horses' hooves as they stopped in the swampy mud to water. Across the sand hills that they must scale on the other side of the river, the mountains, more mountains, lay back against the thunder-heads that awaited the afternoon heat for their delivery. The sun was bright; how bright the sun always turned the after-images when he closed his eyes for a moment!

Nor would be ever forget the snow that visited him his first winter in the Palace, driving the sweet piñon smoke back down the chimneys, muffling the call of the bell from the soldiers' chapel, closing away the mountains for days, and imprisoning the garrison within their mud walls, restless, afraid because there was no way of watching for danger, homesick like little children under the strangeness of the snowfall, for before the storm came, the days had been autumnally golden, sharp in the mornings, and pure with heat at noon.

In those whistling nights, the Captain General sat before his fire, nursing his gray beard over his work table, composing his reports that travelled pages to complete one majestic sentence.

When the snow was falling, with sounds that whispered in the stillness, an unaccustomed gray light was upon the world, the Palace was dark, the tapestries and the brown carved wood gave out no comfort. But when the sun came back, the brilliance was terrible, like an ideal suddenly made plain on the altar, a vision.

The Palace of baked mud, with its low square rooms in endless succession, was coveted. The Captain General scorned the intrigues against him. But they overcame him. He was imprisoned, yielding with a reluctance of soul. Even in his fury, which he disdained to show, he thought how this outrage was only an example of the uncertainty anyone had to face here, and an admonition towards the faith required for triumph.

But the Palace knew him again. The intriguers were put down. He returned, in full command once more, his many names following his title as proudly as his soldiers followed him. The Viceroy and the King heaped him with assurances. He returned to his Palace, he walked in his garden below the high walls, he heard the pleas, he granted the appeals, he strove against famine with yellow corn, he went out again buckled and plated against the marauding Indians.

Once more it was autumn; he knew the sharp scents of those southern mountains in October, when aspens below the timber line turned their yellow leaves, and the pines contributed to the air. His soldiers followed him through the foothills of his domain and into the canyons where shadow and rock seemed to be of the same substance.

Armored, directing a campaign, secure in his valiant past, in a land which was his beloved enemy, he fell ill, was removed to the nearest village of adobe, and there died. For the last time he returned to the Royal City, to be received by God.

He lay under the altar in the soldiers' chapel, a part of the country that, in receiving him, ceased in some degree to be the impassive foe of his kind.

II ——— 1730

THE EVENING AIR

IT COULD BE NOTHING but confusion, though one must hide that, thought the Condesa de Fuentes y Lucientes. She knew that the values of home were struggling to be established here.

The autocracies of God and King must prevail, finally, anywhere.

But in the meantime, she turned her gaze, without opinion, on the Governor's dinner guests. The usual priests, four officers, the wife of one of them, from Mexico City, the cacique of the Indian village—that was really confusing— the German merchant, herself, and her son.

Two women.

Naturally, there was position to maintain.

In and out through the deep, white doorway, the Indian servants carried the food. There were silver platters heaped with chickens, boiled rice, peppered sauces, and hard-boiled eggs carved into garnishings.

The Condesa noticed that the Indian cacique watched the Indian servants with a scowl. He disapproved? Or did he know these servants?

One of them, a small girl with hair cut in a soft bang across her eyebrows, moved with a straight loveliness. Her eyes were downcast. Her mouth lay half open, giving her a stupid look; it quite destroyed a final effect of beauty. The Condesa shrugged; she was overwhelmed by another of the desolations that visited her whenever she remembered the world that lay between her heart and this wretched village of mud.

She was elaborately gowned, her fatly modelled face was overlaid with powder and rouge; she had made no concessions to the primitive society of the Royal City. Her jewels were as magnificent, her aged arrogance as acutely tempered, as if she were in Spain where she belonged, where, with the pomps of attending bishops, she could hold court until death should overtake her fashionably, and she would be carried by eight nobles to a solemn requiem High Mass in a cathedral.

Her hands rested on the table, she fingered the heavy silver fork that was, with its kind, still an innovation to the natives of 1730. Behind her the pretty Indian girl splashed wine into cups of silver.

The Condesa looked at her son.

Had God made her duty plain enough?

As he sat there, listening to an officer, there was a strange mimicry of his dead father in the cut of his features; there was also a disturbing memory of his mother in the calculativeness of his eyes. The Condesa said to herself again that she had done the only thing possible, on receiving the letters.

At the age of sixty-three, with her indignation as the backbone of the strength that brought her across the ocean to Mexico, and thence to the capital of New Mexico, she had come to snatch her last surviving son from the devil. But her duties were heavy, and she groaned with boredom as she gazed around the dining room in the Palace—a row of mud rooms, to be called a Palace!

She had rehearsed her accusations against this new country in the confessional many times. The priest had told her repeatedly that she must not expect too much; this was no longer an age of miracles. If people went into new lands to bring Christ and King, they must expect to wait a few centuries before sin and society were safely and appropriately placed. In the murmur of a Latin absolution, the Condesa had to find what comfort she could. But in her times of bewilderment, when her presence in this mountain capital could hardly be true, after weeks of terrified expectation of death by drowning in a gray-green wave predicted in white foamy ruffles, she was possessed again of her doubts.

And in the person of her son, they found terrible confirmation.

Cipriano de Fuentes y Lucientes, last of four brothers, had joined the Viceroy's train for Mexico in 1724, young enough to desire independence and luxury, and eager enough to pretend that suffering and hardship would dignify these ends. The Viceroy had promised the Condesa a loyal watchfulness, which, in five years, expressed itself in the form of letters whose canon of infamies, disasters, debaucheries, vices (some of which were by him newly invented), depicted to the angry and devout mother what the New World had done to her son. In an effort to surprise him into repentance and salvation, she had sailed for Mexico. The Viceroy, her old friend, directed her to the capital of New Mexico, where her son had gone to Santa Fe on the staff of the Governor. God only knew.

Someone laughed shortly and loudly at the end of the table; the Condesa looked; it was the cacique, who at once went silent again. The candles bloomed steadily in the quiet. The Governor, tiring her with his affectations, assumed for her benefit, began to talk French, with bland ignorance of the limitations of his guests.

In a moment the Indian girl came with a great candelabrum, and stood in the doorway. The Governor arose, gave his arm to the Condesa, and they led the party into the drawing room, where a harp stood, and where the evening air came in through the open windows.

There was still a faint nimbus along the rim of the mountains. That was beautiful. It brought peace. The dark line of the great crest of stone and agedness lay sharp against a lingering pale green, above which the night began in darkness, where the stars' frozen life went forth.

The Condesa sat in a deep red velvet chair, while the officer's wife moved to the harp to play. The Indian cacique was content to look furious and sit quietly.

The Condesa closed her eyes; she looked old and pitiful without their valiant fire. Her throat and bosom were wrinkled and pushed by the severity of her stays. In her powdered wrinkles lay emeralds and diamonds, dusty and magnificent. A little wind sprang up outside and visited her through the window where she sat. She opened her eyes, astonished and moved. The candles dipped and bowed in the breeze, the harp faltered, then spoke on. Her breast was disturbed; the evening air carried on the little wind possessed such sharpness that it was like a memory of delight and remorse to cut her heart in a dream.

She looked around; her son was gone. The intoxications of that wind, bearing the sweet smell of the wood smoke, and the gathered scents of the mountains, of falling streams and fresh ferns, of melting snows through the clear summers, brought the Condesa a vision of the follies its draught must inspire. It was because in her heart she knew that her sacrifice had been unavailing that she now admitted the rise of tears to her eyes. The guests were impassive, through stupidity, she knew; the harp went amateurishly on with its silly melody. She arose, with an imperious nod to command the Governor to let her go alone; grasping at her heavy jewels on her bosom, she stepped through the long door to the stoned floor of the garden that ran behind the Palace. Here was solitude; the wall was high, she could barely see the mountains.

The wind came down across the wall, to stir the few flowers that grew in the garden. The big leaves of the sunflowers scratched along the adobe. Down beyond the dining-room windows, light shone out to the baked ground. It was clear yellow, and travelled as far as the dim orange-colored lantern that hung inside the gateway where the horses and carts of the guests were left.

An ancient bitterness made the Condesa very tired. She walked slowly down the garden, tormenting herself with memories of the serene past, berating herself with the image of her failure. Her son was a depraved wretch; in vain did she plead and lecture and cajole. Pride and position, these were futile as arguments. His name, the meaning of society, the sacred responsibilities of our life in God and of the noble who must be the example for his inferiors—idle. The priest tried to assuage her; he would say that often the older morality collapsed when an old and tried life was put upon another kind of life. But her breast was filled with her two furies; she would strive until she died, in the name of God.

Down by the gateway, in the light, she saw someone moving. She was about to turn, but a laugh betrayed him, and clutching her embroidered gown with her old powdered hands where the dark rings clung like scales, she hastened her step towards the light.

"Cipriano!" she cried, in a voice that achieved only a tortured whisper. Her son turned; he released the Indian servant girl from his arms, and, without surprise or resentment, greeted his mother.

"You are drunk, you are crazy," she said, "I command you to come with me!"

He made a burlesque of a filial tenderness, and turned again to the Indian, who stood silent, her mouth hanging open. He grasped her in his arms again, leaning upon her against the wall. The Condesa felt the touch of despair; and she knew that death was the brother of that visitor.

She pulled back her heavy sleeves, and took from the ground by the gate a whip with three thongs of rawhide.

Her tears began to flow.

She raised her arm and called upon the Holy Ghost for grace.

She made the sign of the cross, her jewels sparkling dimly in the carriage lantern light, and crashed the whip across the striving lovers with a final strength.

III   1780

TRIUMPHAL ENTRY

THE CRY OF THE BELLS came winging across the Royal City, as the sun reached the zenith and shone upon all things equally, the mountains crested in white, the tiny valley of the river, the roofs of the town.

There was high excitement in the people.

Early in the morning, scouts had come riding from the edge of Labajada to report that the Bishop's train was visible, the entry could be expected about noon.

The old brass cannon in the plaza before the Palace pumped the glory of this visit, its concussion knocking its fuse-holder down. In all the streets they had flung out flags and cloths, bright stuffs that caught the morning wind in jubilee. In the windows were candles, waiting to be lighted. The women had assumed their finest gowns and mantillas, and the men aggrandized the martial accoutrements of their costume with silver buttons and doeskin leggings. The altar of the soldiers' chapel was a glory of gold and silver and flowers—roses made from painted corn husks, fastened to dyed green willow twigs. The friars had worked for weeks. On the holy stone was laid the only piece of gold lace in their treasury.

[15]

The cannon was fired again.

In through the narrow lanes of the streets the answering salutes came from the Bishop's escort. It was not long before the procession appeared. Horsemen goaded their animals to a plunging gait, the horses rolled their agate eyes in a stunning frenzy, the hymn of delight was taken up on all sides, the people shrieked with satisfaction. A cavalcade in armor and velvet preceded the carriages. These soldiers, exquisite in spite of their travel which had cost them no fighting, were proudly ignorant of the screaming girls who ran by their sides. They were followed by a long cart covered with hides, drawn by several mules. Bowing with satisfaction from its interior were the Bishop's personal attendants and lesser ecclesiastics.

And at last, the carriage of the Bishop himself.

This was a tremendous, airy vehicle pulled by eight mules; its interior was plainly visible—the Bishop sat revealed between his leather curtains which were rolled back. He sat with his chaplain, a Jesuit in military uniform. He made the sign of benediction every few feet, smiling upon the people that threatened his carriage wheels every step of the way. Its cushions were of brocaded blue velvet; an ivory crucifix hung facing the Bishop. Behind and above were piled the leather hampers full of vestments and ceremonial plate, the costumes of pomp and the vessels of celebration.

Beside the episcopal equipage rode the Governor of New Mexico on his white horse. His pride matched that of his people, but he disdained to show it.

The procession came into the plaza, where the brass cannon had been reduced to a smudged relic by the zeal of its attendants. The bells still sent flocks of the birds of jubilee over the city.

In the furious sunlight that pierced but did not heat the air, the Bishop stepped from his carriage with the assistance of his chaplain, turned once to bless the crowd, and entered the Palace with the Governor.

The people broke around the carriages to examine them, to exclaim over the silver-studded caparisons of the mules, the copper and gold hammered into the great spokes, the beautiful paintings on the panels of the doors and on the wide leather springs which had supported the Bishop in his tremendous journey from his See in Mexico.

The bells cried a final paean, dying with echoes that ringed the plaza until silence held the early afternoon.

Later in the day, rumors went around.

The Bishop was resting. He had said that the zeal of the people was a glory to God. The Governor was a man whose might was qualified by goodness. The magnificence of the Palace was as comfortable as it was astonishing. The chaplain was empowered to say for His Lordship that it was indeed a great honor to be the first Bishop to visit the Royal City.

In the late afternoon, the chaplain put off his military uniform and took from his servant who was unpacking his leather hamper a cassock, which he put on. Then, secretly amused by the fury of preparations that these provincials were making in the city and in the Palace, he walked through the long galleries filled with girls and servants polishing silver, fabricating triumphal flowers with their utmost ingenuity, gossiping in ecstacy about the Bishop; and he came out into the garden, where two fruit trees lifted their young branches and created a hint of shade. In his hand he carried his breviary. The Bishop was asleep. There was time before the Angelus for a reverie or a prayer. He sat down on the carved wooden bench below the trees.

[17]

It was fortunate that the Bishop had been pleased by his reception. The situation was exquisite at best; for him to come overland with a meagre train those many hundred miles to subjugate the Franciscans who refused to recognize his episcopal authority, this was no trifle. Incredible, that there should be two points of view about the matter; yet it was known that the Franciscans were stubborn, they had founded the missions in the land, theirs the glory and the power.

The chaplain, who was a Jesuit from Spain with the complexion of the late eighteenth century upon his mind, moulded of skepticism and opportunism, intelligence and faith, opened his book and found his hours, but closed it when he saw pacing under the wall, at the far end of the garden, a Franciscan monk whose head was sunk within his lowered cowl.

The chaplain arose, gathering his fine cassock about him to lift it above the sharp dust, and went to the other priest with an idea of testing local opinion as to the magnificent entry at noon.

He saw that his companion in prayer was past middle age, wretched in a robe of frayed wool, with rags at its hem dragging in the dust. From the weathered, burnt face grew a beard thick with gray. The Franciscan's eyes were weak from sunlight and disaster witnessed. He waited for the Jesuit to speak.

"You permit me to greet you?" said the chaplain.

"I am finishing my prayers," replied the monk.

"And I."

The Jesuit fell in with the slow pace of the monk; they walked back and forth in the blue shadow of the wall, silent, neither praying, yet reluctant to begin the duel which their meeting must bring.

At last the Franciscan, with simple straightforwardness, crossed himself, and replaced his hands inside his crossed sleeves. The chaplain coughed with formality, also crossed himself, and with a sudden movement of tact, dropped his cassock so that it dragged in the dirt.

The monk kindled.

"You are too polite," he said. "That is fine cloth to drag in our dirt."

"No, no, no," said the Jesuit, "if we are speaking in allegories, Father, I must say that our fine cloth is vanity and the dirt is God's earth, where the highest must finally be lowered."

"I have tasted every kind of dust and dirt in this kingdom," said the Franciscan. "I have saved hundreds of souls. I have never ridden in a painted carriage with gold and leather springs. Nor have I desired to possess anything that I and my brothers have not earned."

The chaplain was excited and happy that the monk was so immediately full of grievance. The Bishop would be the better able to prepare for it if this temper were sampled beforehand.

"Authority," he said, rolling his eyes out of sight for a second like the Bishop in the flood of a sermon, "is a sublime thing, we must all bow to its saving grace."

"Usurped authority," said the monk in the toneless voice of resignation, "is glory to no one."

They turned at the garden wall and paced towards the Palace, where the dinner for that evening was engaging six cooks.

"It is inevitable," he continued. "For more than a century my brotherhood has baptized, buried, and nursed, and consoled these people. Our tongues have hung with famine. Our souls have been lost and regained through exhaustion and temptation. We have gone in rags to the rich man and the poor man alike. Our work is never done; it is taken for granted—we are no longer miracles sent from heaven to succor and save the people. The country is changing. My Lord Bishop is the final conquest, we are overwhelmed."

The Jesuit turned his head away in embarrassment from the fierce light in those weak eyes; he smiled in his heart, at such passion, and approved impartially.

"It is true that goodness is a positive quality in mankind," he said at last, "but let us not conclude that there is only one kind of goodness. I assure you that my Lord Bishop, whom you hate so, is a great and good man. You have been generous in your preparations; the people are full of zeal. It is a beautiful city. Some day it must have a cathedral—"

The Franciscan gestured rudely with his heavy sleeves.

"Forgive me, Father," he said, "if I leave you to finish my prayers. You recognize the bitterness in my heart; grant me leave to go and banish it."

The Jesuit bowed. "I had hoped we might understand our differences so thoroughly that they would disappear!" he said, with a smile.

"They will disappear," said the Franciscan. "You are the eighteenth century, I am the sixteenth, already I am late, very late."

He turned and strode to the other end of the garden, where he took up, in the full late sunlight, the walking of prayer.

The chaplain was inclined to a certain tenderness—it was so simple a defeat, there was so little honor in bagging a foe who was rational with despair.

The sun was crimson in its descent, dusk was near, the mountains lay in the glow of rose.

From the soldiers' chapel the Angelus rang out; the chaplain and the Franciscan at opposite ends of the garden sank to their knees. Within the Palace the cooks halted their work, the servants bowed before the silver they polished, the Bishop knelt in his bedroom by the side of his leather trunks, whose lids were open, revealing the copes of white silk and gold, of blue velvet starred in rose diamonds, the mitre of gold kid leather edged with pearls, the chasubles in gold and silver with holy images embroidered and painted, the satin slippers with gold crosses, the white linen undervestments worked with lace, the scarlet cassocks of ceremony, and the velvet wrappings that contained the jewelled chalice, monstrance, and ciborium which accompanied the Bishop wherever he went, even to the farthest and most outlandish town in his domain.

IV ——————— 1846
BITTERSWEET WALTZ

THEY COULD HARDLY KNOW they were creating a romantic tradition in 1846. The land looked the same as it had looked for centuries. The sunlight washed along the walls of the Old Palace with ageless splendor, and as the American troops drew closer and closer, ignoring the fatuous proclamations of the Governor and the lieutenants he sent on horseback with majestic threats, the epoch was in its dying fall.

In the stove room of the United States Hotel, opposite the Palace, there was much competent talk. It was the commercial element that devised the wholly mythical fate of the Mexican Governor and his court; nothing could be too dreadful as an end for that querulous tyrant, whose infamies lacked the saving grace of style, whose character dwelt in braggadoccio and was betrayed in cowardice. It is true that guitars, and serenades, and flashing white teeth, eagerly indiscreet passion, and the rest of the racial marks of life in the Royal City, were exciting. But to the accompaniment of murder and robbery, farcical attempts at justice, these things lost desirability. Levi Wurzburg, with the other men of his age and trade, was more than delighted when General Kearny answered the Governor's latest threat by reading it, smiling, and continuing the march from Las Vegas.

And when the long columns of blue soldiers on horseback halted outside the city to receive the surrender from the Lieutenant Governor (for his chief, who had fled, clutching his riches to his stomach in the last throes of indignity), Levi was on hand to dance and throw his hat, and scream hoarse welcome to the American soldiers.

General Kearny received the Lieutenant Governor with good manners, gave a command, and the cavalry moved into the Royal City as owners for the American government.

Once again the streets were lined by speculative eyes as the sun-colored soldiers rode by. The women estimated the tempers and the susceptibilities of the invaders: there were old eyes full of resentment that invasion had occurred, particularly at such a tragic time of life as their own; there were young eyes full of the reversible promises that the ladies of that race always made to their conquerors. General Kearny's soldiers felt the sting of the mountain air; when they drew up in formation in the plaza while the General read his proclamation of amnesty and martial law, there was something agreeable about the prospect of staying in the town for a while.

In the evening there was a dinner at the Palace. The General and his officers sat down with the Lieutenant Governor and some of the substantial citizens, among whom Levi Wurzburg had earned his right to be included. His neighbors thought of him as a merchant prince. His wife, a Spaniard of a shrewdness that matched his own, brought her ancient inherited graces to the business of abetting his eminence. After dinner, Señora Wurzburg and her daughters were in front of the Palace.

With an honorable tenacity, Levi managed to bring General Kearny away from the party long enough to meet his wife and children. It was a classic moment, which he described as one to be remembered and told to properly respectful descendants. General Kearny assisted Levi in making it a socially successful occasion, and the Wurzburg girls were ravished by the charm of the conqueror, while their mother stood fingering her black laces, her heavy gold brooches, her faint mustache, her heavy wrinkled jaws.

The light from inside the Palace bathed them all in a dim splendor.

Across the plaza, jubilee sounded in the United States Hotel; the soldiers and the local wits were relaxing. Bonfires turned the mud houses a gallant orange in the blue night.

Levi was full of a bowel-changing happiness; there would now be American rule, his business was safe forever, there would be happier times for the family, with officers, and eventually, a new society.

An aide came out of the Palace and reported that General Kearny's presence was requested inside by the Lieutenant Governor.

The General bowed to Señora Wurzburg; his heavy epaulettes showered forward across his blue shoulders. He bowed to the Señoritas Wurzburg, and then, turning, with an afterthought, presented his aide, Brevet Captain Duncan.

The young man bowed and shook hands, unaware of the sharp fury of Señora Wurzburg's regard, as she drew her black lace across her face, leaving only her eyes that now looked remote and dynamic, as if they generated some fire of resentment and classification. With an automatic movement, she grasped the waist of her younger child, drew her away, and was reaching for the older, when Captain Duncan offered his arm for a promenade down the long pillared portal of the Palace. Leah Wurzburg put her little hand in the clothy crook of his elbow, and went with him, loudly admiring the imminent stars.

Mornings of full summer gold saw the new flag rise over the Palace, and evenings that fell upon the scarcely completed dusk saw that flag come down.

The month of August went by in a glory of readjustments; September came, and the aspens up the canyon began to taste the sharp frosty air of early morning with the presage of wintry decline. Enthusiasm was contagious; the Royal City accelerated its gaieties; there seemed to be a nostalgia from the fine tragic history of the past mingled with the bright promises of this new future, whose symbols were the soldiers, a rough caste of men, yet for all their national rowdiness, honest and innocently so, without any virtuous awareness of honesty such as the Latin often felt.

The moment seemed to have such a bright newness that it was almost a mockery of the ancient land on which it rested.

Who could judge the values or romanticism that then came together, first in conflict, then in hybrid confusion?

The bells still rang out at morning and evening, circling the Royal City with their calls like white doves, the guitars still thumped like faintly ridiculous hearts beating, the dance was still the fandango, and still the *vals despacioso*, though it was a stimulating pleasure to learn the Missouri breakdown from these soldiers, who laughed all the time, even when a jealous husband or lover made the signs of pugnacity with teeth, dagger, and curse.

On the last night, the officers got no sleep at all.

The General allowed a ball to be given.

Violinists came from Las Vegas, Albuquerque, all the cities that could contribute to the orchestra. There were three harps, eleven violins, a violoncello, and a flute. In that night of late September, they engendered music that was like the blood of happiness. A thousand candles with crystals and silver lighted the long old rooms, one after the other in straight succession. The windows were open, the Palace was a pavilion of romance and music where the army of occupation danced for the last time with the girls of the Royal City.

In exactly the nick of time, one of Levi Wurzburg's wagon trains had arrived from Mexico City with the latest gowns from Paris. There was one of cream-colored satin for Leah; she wore it with her heart revealed in the style of the madonnas her mother revered. In her hair, which was pulled upward from her sweet nape and piled widely about her ears, she wore two diamond combs that had belonged to a great Vicereine in the old days. In her hands she carried a small fan painted with *amorini*. In her eyes she carried a tragic satisfaction that if to-morrow came, to-day had come before it.

Brevet Captain Duncan came for her very properly in the only coach in town, one that was often used to carry the sacraments in, one that Captain Duncan had achieved by bribery and corruption.

All the night long the dance went on; in the cry of the violins and the rills of melody from the harps, like brook water tumbling across little stones, in the shuffle of feet across the difficult board floors of the Palace, in the tiny clanging of spurs, in the laughter, and in the moan of the 'cello when the slow waltz, the *vals despacioso*, was played, the morning's sharp arrival with bugle and drum was dreaded.

If the General took his departure shortly after midnight, his officers understood that it was because someone must be awake to start on the long journey to-morrow, to California. For the rest, there would never be another night like this: never such girls with mouths like wild strawberries, sweet, desirable, and warm, who offered themselves in the slow waltz to a bittersweet abandon as brief and as enduring as the inciting wind that travelled in the night from the mountains, as the call of the violins and the harps in that long vista of candle-lighted rooms, where the uniform turned with the black lace, the cream-colored satin, the scarlet mantillas, the roses, the diamond eardrops—

Such things had a value that was perhaps enriched by the arrival of dawn across the mountains.

The flute was stilled, the violins with backs like the polished coat of a fine horse, the swanlike harps, were set in the corner.

In the dusty assembly of the troops, the bugle cracked the morning air with orders. Saddles and equipment creaked and clashed.

The flag was up, casting its watery shadow on the Old Palace.

A voice cried an order; the blue column moved out and was wished Godspeed by the ladies of the Royal City.

They stood in ball dress in the early sunlight, waving.

V   1878
FROCK COATS & the LAW

I**T WAS** an elegant railroad car that brought the new Governor of the Territory as far as Trinidad, Colorado. In 1878 it was still necessary to leave that gold and plush carriage, with its filigreed oil lamps, carved partitions, velvet draperies edged with bolero bangles, at the Colorado line, and continue the journey to the capital of New Mexico by buckboard, two days and one night.

In the pocket of his frock coat that was made of thick broadcloth, General Wallace carried his preliminary reports. The President, also clad in a frock coat and broadcloth trousers that looked tubular, like stove pipe, dull black with formal wrinkles, had sent a soldier, a General of the Civil War, to bring order to the bleak land where the murderous cattle war was flourishing.

An exact epitome of his time, the new Governor arrived with a war record, an established growth of whiskers, a knowledge of quotable Latin, and the partly finished manuscript of a tremendous novel, subtitled "A Tale of the Christ." He rode into the city in his overland buckboard, drove around the plaza, saw the Exchange Hotel a block west of the Cathedral, and the painted sign atop a saloon absurdly reading "Take a Gin Fiz," and finally pulled up at the Palace of the Governors.

Another siege had opened within those aged walls.

General Wallace found a city of narrow streets, lined with low adobe houses, inscrutable with small windows, the frames painted a convivial blue.

He had learned something of the history of the Royal City before coming to inhabit its Palace.

He found that the ancient Spanish graces were gone; it was easy enough to believe in the traditions of the Castilian nobility who once had moved in the society there; but few enough of its traces survived. Nor could he honestly report to President Hayes or Mr. Secretary Schurz that what he had found as his new capital was a truly American city. What there was of the United States there, was compounded of pioneer ways that had solemn virtues, and of outlaw manners that had equally solemn dangers. For the rest, the inner life of the people, the unfinished Cathedral, and the strife of the Archbishop against obstacles of distance and languidness no doubt sufficed.

Concerned with the manuscript of a Methodist epic, he sat up in the light of a student lamp until late at night, in an old arm chair with faded velvet cushions, holding a writing board across his knees while the pen poured out page after page of "Ben Hur."

But his daytimes were busy with investigation and report.

The outrages to the south, where the cattle war went on, presently took on concentration in a single ideal figure; out of the welter of thieves and murderers and convicts that formed the majority of the fighters, a boy appeared and at once achieved a popular renown that was vigorous enough to oppose that of the Governor.

William Bonney was a little fellow and he was called Billy the Kid. He stood for his photograph against a sunlightcd adobe wall, his hat on the back of his rough head, his eyes pale, his mouth open showing small teeth that lifted the lip slightly, his short arms by his side, holding in his small hands the firearms of his trade. There was no record on the film of the instant efficacy he was capable of.

People never believed that Billy Bonney was really a smart assassin until they saw him or his victims.

General Wallace, nursing his beard and "Ben Hur" through long studious nights, sent messages of Christian hope to the terrorized county; amnesty would follow a full confession of sins and a promise to do better.

Oaths of scorn were the answers.

Mrs. Wallace, Susan, came out the year after to join the Governor in the Old Palace, which horrified her by its dilapidation—the ceiling sagged, the boards of the floor were laid directly upon the hardened earth. How strange the horsehair sofas of the period looked against the white-washed walls! Yet (for she was a woman of taste) how handsome, once it became familiar as a style.

If the General had found the place socially bleak, his wife was even more disappointed.

It was sometimes agreeable to gather with certain of the ladies of the town in the afternoon, either in the Palace or in one of the mansions further up Palace Avenue, such as the Staab house, with its yellow and white stone, its deep lawns with iron animals and weeping willows, its sombre elegances in the more acceptable style of the English Queen. On such occasions, Susan Wallace heard charming stories of the old days: how romantic it was in the time of the American military occupation in the 1840's, with the picnics, the balls at Fort Marcy, the parades, the liveliness that a garrison of officers must always bring.

And stories of an even earlier time—an ancient lady, in black lace with gold brooches enamelled in black, could remember such prodigies of romance as duels and deaths behind the soldiers' chapel, vast state dinners like the one they had when one of the Bishops of Durango came from Mexico, and elopements across the prairies on swift horses, with pursuit in the form of a cavalcade on silver saddles.

Mrs. Wallace was tactful—the colors of the past meant much to these ladies; and she saved her complaints for the letters she wrote home.

The only diversions were reading and listening to the band concerts on Sunday evenings. The plaza was crowded with buggies; they came from ranches in the surrounding country, and from the carriage houses of the rich people in Palace Avenue. The Mexicans, unaffectedly happy in their best clothes, made each concert a *fiesta*. The girls, practising inherited arts of flirtation, circled the bandstand in one direction, walking in sodalities of opinion. The boys, early matured with wise eyes and small mustaches, walked in the opposite direction around the band which strove with "The Alhambra Gavotte de Concert." There was constant exchange of messages, and the horses neighed, babies wailed.

Mrs. Wallace was sure it must be a unique spectacle—one that had elements of prettiness in it—though Lew detested the band.

While she wrote her letters, describing their trips into the warring territory with humor and bravery, the General contrived to have President Hayes declare an Insurrection in New Mexico; and four troops of cavalry began active operations. The citizens were relieved; they felt that victory over the desperadoes would close forever any such outbreaks of murder and theft.

There were two kinds of self-righteousness, that of the outlaw, of Billy the Kid, which saw itself as the instrument of personal justice and revenge; and that of the frock-coated Governor and his tremendous significance as the type of government.

The frock coat prevailed with the law in two months— "and at the end of that time the desperadoes were driven out of the country, armed factions were broken up, and the best grazing section of country in the United States was opened to immigrants," wrote the Governor.

So he contributed to the chronicle of change that makes all history.

He loved the air in Santa Fe, the sunlight which was so clear and so full of promise that such weather must last forever.

It was easy, out of doors, to forget the outlandish things that crossed his private and official path at every step, it was even easier to forget them in his writing room, where he closed himself in, night after night, with the student lamp.

The manuscript grew; he worked sometimes ten hours at a time, though Susan was troubled for fear of his betrayal by that very lamp he used to see by.

She wrote home that Billy the Kid was heard to remark, "I intend to ride into the plaza at Santa Fe, hitch my horse in front of the Palace, and put a bullet through Lew Wallace."

He would then surrender and be hanged. Susan thought that the lamp threw too clear a silhouette of her husband on the window—what if that tragically foolish boy from Lincoln actually rode up and attempted to prove what a great man he was? She closed the shutters herself.

And when she went back east, she made him promise to do the same.

But she had not long to worry; a competent sheriff shot William Bonney one night in a dark room.

"Ben Hur" was nearly finished; the railroad was coming closer and closer, and at last it reached Santa Fe.

There were celebrations.

General Wallace realized that now it was really gone—that time of which they all talked in the Royal City—when the life of town and land was of necessity intensely local and independent. He wrote under his lamp; the shutters were open to the black sky that faded to a mysterious glow, down at the edge of the mountains. Presently he was able to write to Susan that the long book was done; he would soon be home with her. There would be no more of those solitary nights beside his lamp, with the night made melancholy by the call of the engine whistles from the railroad, a new sound.

Before, only the sound of bells in the church towers had fallen over the Palace and the whole of the Royal City.

TWO:

TAOS
VALLEY

I   1772

THE FORTRESS

FOR God Who lived in man was, indeed, embattled. The church, therefore, needed to be not only God's roof but His children's. The Franciscan kept this in mind while he worked at the drawings. He had fifteen sheets of the most beautiful parchment which he had brought from Mexico, which his cousin, who was a professor of canon law at the University of Salamanca in Spain, had sent to him by ship four years ago. He had never touched the beautiful cream-colored surface until now. There had been ideas for prayers and devotions which he had been tempted to write down; but instead he had contented himself with rehearsing them in his mind. Something had told him not to use the paper yet. Accordingly it had come, rolled in a tube, all the way up the Rio Grande with him. In his pouch, too, he had some dried sprigs of *guizache*, which, when wetted and distilled, made a passable ink—one that blended nicely with the charcoal that he always liked to use for preliminary sketching.

He told them all what he was about, but they were Indians, and they seemed to have entirely different purposes for the art of drawing from his. He conceded that their pueblos—

those two long houses of rising cubes of earthen rooms which faced each other in front of Taos mountain—certainly did not have the look of anything planned out beforehand. And yet (this was curious) the houses had a look of balance and design which made him set his head on one side and squint at them, to see how the triangles of shadow and the squares of sunlighted clay rose from the ground in a nicety of order.

They watched all his processes.

They went along when he went to find some quills, and when they understood what he was after, they smiled, and sent a boy, who came back with a handful of the most magnificent eagle feathers you could hope for. He sharpened these, slit them, licked them, and scraped off the soft white barbs for an inch or so to give his fingers a grip. They watched him soak his *guizache* sprigs, and make that dark brown tea which, when it settled and could be poured off until a proper density was made, became a useful ink. They saw him hold his first sheet of parchment up to the sunlight, and they marvelled at the richness and still the thinness of the skin, and then he spread it down on a smoothed board he had found leaning on one of the bake ovens at the pueblo, and spiked it in place with thick cactus thorns. He had some slivers of charcoal which he pointed by rubbing them on a flat stone. The little crowd around him watched his hands, and at everything the hands did, they would lift their eyes and consult his face to see *what*.

He said to himself that they were going to build it with their hands, and therefore, they should see every step of the process.

The Franciscan was a small fellow, with a grainy and muscular body that was as tough as dried meat on a rawhide line out behind any of the pueblo houses. The plains, the

enormous river journey on foot, the upping and the downing
of mountains, the garment of God's weather, had made him
into this leathery man of middle years, whose vanity had
long ago been left behind with other childish substitutes for
good deeds. He was shortly bearded, and there was gray in
his whiskers. The under-porches of his brows were pale,
where the sun never reached, because his eyes were deep set
and he squinted habitually against the powers of the light,
both within his mind and without. His brows shadowed his
surprisingly blue eyes with youthful candor; as shadows in
this whole land were full of reflected glow. His tonsure was
rough-grown again. He had long since passed from the reach
of a reverend barber. Everybody watching him always came
back to looking at his hands, though. They were rough, scaly,
veined like a tree, with broken nails, and knobby joints; but
how delicately they moved, and how surely, and when he
spoke or prayed or said Mass, how full of knowledge and
reference his hands seemed!

He had a general idea of what the church would be like. It
would naturally be built, like the other missions of New Mexico, out of earth and timber. It would take the shape of a huge
cross on the ground. That was usual enough, and a design
which could not be improved upon, for the very meaning of
the building was so told in its shape on the ground.

Yes, well, but there were one or two other things to think of.

The Apaches and Comanches had been by this way many
a time. The Pueblos themselves had once arisen and mur-
dered all Spaniards. Even now, the Indians who lived here—
right in these rancherias, where the new church would be
built, the place spoken of as Ranchos de Taos—though they
were polite and curious, these Indians did not seem actually
seized with the love of God and need of Him in their hearts.

He knew that he could talk to them, and that they understood exactly what he had to say to them. In the exchange of their eyes, he sometimes felt, peacefully, but quite powerfully, how they measured their hundreds against his one; and the notion of his death was never very far from his mind, because he read it so commonly in the comings and goings of thought, even of a certain propriety, in the Indian faces.

So the church had to be a fortress, too.

And then, what had he seen in the country itself? How rains came off the mountains and made rivers, embracing whole plains, where the flood waters could open out and spread and cut vagrant gullies in the soft desert earth, changing shape after shape, of plain and hill and cliff.

So if a church were built in a land under such heavenly tempers, how could it hope to stand, when erosion wore away the red faces of stone cliffs, unless it were made strong, and twice strong, and thrice strong?

And another thing. Without vanity, he knew that he had power. He did not consider it his own, but God's, and it was used for God's purposes, too, and altogether. He believed in his Franciscan brothers. But he knew too that weakness may appear anywhere. What would happen if the next one who came to preach and work here had his heart set otherwise? What if there was such a thing as erosion of the spirit, too? There might be. Perhaps the next, or the next, or the one after him, might neglect the church, and the rains would wash, and the mud would melt, and little rivers would begin down from the roof, and the clay would cave gently here, and settle there, and the ground would curve up against the walls, and the ancient process of earth returning to earth would have yet another illustration, which could be arrested only if later men continued to build and rebuild, so that the walls would keep growing in expected weathers. To guard against another's weakness, long after himself, the walls would need to be strong.

And besides, he ruefully admitted, with the rude implements available here, there could hardly be anything else but a rough and hardy structure.

All these reasons were in his thoughts as he made his drawings. They stayed by him as bitter truths as he led the people of the rancherias to work. They made their cross on the ground, one hundred and twenty feet long, and half as wide from arm to arm. The walls must be high enough to mean something in the spirit. There would be two towers for bells, in front. He tried to stay awake sometimes to know all things about the church in advance, and the fancy that charmed him the most was the one of how the great cast bells would sound at night, when there was wind, and everything else so still, that the rim-song of the bells as the wind blew across their open mouths would be sweet, faint, yet plain to anyone wanting to hear.

He could not measure the days it took to go from the drawings on the Salamanca parchment to the mud, the blocks of stone, the hewn timbers, on the ground at the Ranchos de Taos. When they said how thick should the walls be, at the base, he came and stood on the line which was marked out on the ground. It was the line corresponding to the inner wall of the church as he had it in the drawings. He took a full pace outward, and then another, and then after a pause, another; raked his loose sandal heel on the ground, and said here. Nine feet wide! Yes, he said, that wide, and ground his teeth and put out his lower lip, in a sort of ugly magnificence, if they didn't think he knew what he was about.

So they built it that way, but when the walls were laid, and had begun to rise, he was not satisfied. They had such weight that their power would tend downward, maybe outward. He had seen land wear away. A cliff that lasted always had hills behind it. He ordered more dirt, and still more; and began to build buttresses like hills against the corners where the walls angled and joined. The others could not see why, nor could he tell them, but he knew by the same reason of his eye which had made some lines in the drawings thus long, and some others in relation, thus longer.

As it evolved, he would go off a little way and see it in all lights of day and night. It did look as if God's rough hand had come down from Heaven and cleaved off all the earth about the church, cutting straight down here to release a wall, and straight down there, and by such great cuts and removals, revealing the shape of the recumbent cross in towering relief, out of the blind ground itself.

But there was one trouble with that notion, and it made his heart heavy the nearer they came to the finish. Remembering churches in Mexico, and in Spain, both real and painted, and their lacy aspirations, their delicacy, the elegance of their open buttresses and spires and the exquisite flight of their use of curved lines, the jewelled twilights of their windows, he said to himself that his church, though it might stand for a time, and save lives, and shelter God, had no beauty.

He looked at his hands, and recalled the fine tools used by skilled craftsmen on the churches of his envy. Pah!

But in the name of one who knew how to do something with nothing, he named it the Mission of Saint Francis of Assisi.

In final humility, he never knew that the beauty of his purposes and reasons went into the walls three paces thick, the roof like a canyon rim, the buttresses like foothills, the light and shadow of a mesa; and was there to be seen ever after.

II 1831

TAOS LIGHTNING

THE FIRST THING François Labardie wanted to do when he reached Taos by nightfall of this day, November ninth, 1831, was to get warm, all through, both sides of him, top and bottom, and inside, in his crust-like hollow belly. In the mountains, by the cold-cracked rocks, it was possible to make a fire and blister your front or your back; but never were you warm generally, all over, at one and the same time. It took a room and a fireplace and some of that blazing hot sauce they made in Taos, and a jug of that whisky called Taos Lightning, which was admitted to be the milk of a pregnant wildcat kitty in which her claws could be tasted going down the throat, so that to enjoy and cure the drink required the loudest yell a man could make, no matter where he might be at the moment.

François was a heavy young man from Louisiana in his third year as a trapper in the Rocky Mountains. He wooed the solitude of his labors with the kind of love that it was embarrassing to explain to anyone else. He knew comfortably that there were plenty of others like him, and so felt anything but unique or heroic in what he did. He was one of the smartest animals in the whole immense mountain system: an animal with more equipment than the beavers, the foxes, the yellow cats; the young cinnamon bears and the velvet-skinned deer; the silver wolf of the high canyons—among whom he made his living. In his thoughts he could talk the conversation of these animals, both proposing and answering all voices of the dialogue. His thoughts he lived aloud, when he was alone in the mountains. Sometimes the habit was odd, if not trouble-making, when he was back in town and speaking simply what was in his mind.

Having come to the mountains by his own choice, and having found what he sought, he was happy there. He sometimes wondered how people who lived anywhere else ever managed to know themselves, and how they decided what they wanted, or needed, or believed to be good.

For months at a time he would be off in the rocks, absorbed and invisible in a world of dark green pine and silver stone walls; high meadows where the noon winds carried carpets of scent from one field of wild flowers to another, which bloomed so vividly the higher he climbed, until at ten thousand feet, where the white-headed eagles lived, and the most sumptuous of timber wolves, the flowers were colored like jewels, and almost burned with light in the sharp air. For his own life, he fished in the rivers, which came like the vital essence of the rocks out of the mountain groins. He fell into the rivers to bathe when the sun was direct on the white water; and cold, the water cut something out of him that he could spare, any softness of flesh or spirit, and he arose cleaned and confirmed and cousin to the trout he grasped at in the speckled clear river. Who else had a bed of moss to lie on for hours watching a trap, watching for the first delicate tread of a furred paw out of a mist of forest leaves, blue with morning?

How cunningly the paw tried, trod, and walked, until the whole creature was in view! How silent the creature and the trapper, both! The silence was lorded over by the wind ever so high in the tallest fingers of the pines, where a cloud-like music was caught and chorded. Whole days went past in which such music took the place of human thought, and the words he spoke aloud were, to François, only other forest sounds.

During the trapping months, he visited his caches, and saw his riches grow; and when they had come to such scale as was God's limit upon them, which meant all he could carry, his strength having been given him, limited, and ordained of God, it was often the time when the snow began to visit the mountains at night. A certain kind of cloud simply began to drop itself vastly and intimately upon all things, and the cloud's nature was the snow itself. It could be scented, if the head was turned just right, and the eyes shut the better to smell what the day or the night would bring.

Then the cycle of perfection would come once again around its course in François' character, and there would begin to live in his head, his heart, his belly, his loins, this desire for warmth, which for all these months of both heat and cold, sun, rain, and flower and river, had been buried deep inside him. It would come first as a dream: sleeping, he would stir to the memory of warmth of all those kinds; and he would see himself coming back daily more and more to feeling like a man instead of like an especially gifted animal; and now and then it would strike him with a pang that he was in hazardous life, that the mountains were really enemy to him, after all, and that a law of spirit among his own kind included such a thing as fear.

He would long for warmth and excitement and other men

and women. The mountain water would feel hot when he broke ice and splashed his face at a river pool or a high meadow lake. He would have to see a barber and have this black shiny mask taken off his red cheeks. He would have to oil his hair and scrape the pine-smelling sap out of it, and he would buff his teeth with salt at the house of Señora Abeyta where he liked to stay in Taos, and when he would smile, he would flash black and white and red at the candle-lighted table. He would sing songs again, of which he remembered many. He would tell stories, and put the words into the mouths of the mountain animals, so that they would all die laughing to hear him speaking with the voice of Monsieur Fox, and Capitaine Wolf, and Père Yellowcat, and Mademoiselle Gazelle. Such delights would flood him, and hurry him back towards Taos, and he would know once more, only by the act of seasonal thought, how loneliness could change everything: all accustomed joys; until they seemed, he supposed, actually savage.

What it meant was that anything less than total observance of the terms of the mountains would result in failure and death. Admission of loneliness would be, however slight, a fatal degree. Only on the way down the slopes towards the vast yellow plain could this be admitted. Dark green trees against the snowy ground turned into a general blue wall of mountain as he left them behind, and toiled towards nightfall and the sunset colored lights that began to show and stay in the windows of the mud village, otherwise invisible in the earth shadow.

They knew him, at several places, as he came into town. The plaza was spotted with light and music. Across from Señora Abeyta's house was the saloon that had the wooden floor, wide planks which sprang a little when they were danced upon. He would appear there later in the evening, and feel the boards spring beneath his capering feet, probably the pleasantest feeling in the world.

It was an epic warmth that stole through him, then, that ninth of November, in 1831. By ten in the evening, he was full of fiery food, and the room where he sat with friends was glowing like a little furnace. The mud-plastered walls held the heat and baked it back upon them all.

It was a sharp, damp night, outside, mist was hovering down the canyon. There was nothing like such a night out to make a toasty room feel like heaven. François poured the Taos whisky down his throat and cried and yelled at the claws of the ghostly panther that raked his voice as it gurgled down. There were two Abeyta daughters and they both sat with him and screamed the songs he taught them and blew their cigarettes down his neck. They slapped him at hearing of what Monsieur Fox said when the white-headed eagle stripped him of his elegant golden breeches. They went with him to dance across the plaza and he was complimented by the verses made and sung in his honor by Don Sixto and the other musician. The floor thundered and shook under him. Everybody stood in a ring and clapped while he danced with the two Abeytas and nobody else. He had come down from the mountains like spring in autumn, and Taos was warm and the whisky was begetting cat-cleverness in his head and there was fire in his arms and he swung the girls, and the candles made a little hot wind and the clay walls were covering him kindly and the music talked to him, right here, in this ear, and who knew so well as François Labardie how good such things were, while they lasted, in that little mud town so far from everything everywhere else?

The WESTERN ATTORNEY

IME AND AGAIN he thanked his stars for the document folded in the oilskin wallet carried in the breast pocket of his magnificently cut broadcloth coat, which was pale gray with brown velvet facings and silver buttons. Except for the paper, it was likely that they'd've made him walk, or ride one of those absurd small Western horses. As it was, the equipage was not too dismal: an army ambulance, detached from the main column bound for Fort Union, and sent on from Raton through the Cimarron Canyon with him, until he should be safely (if not comfortably!) deposited in Taos as the new Assistant to the United States Attorney for the Territory of New Mexico—a term which began herewith in the spring of 1852.

If the books could be trusted, he was coming to a vivid and dangerous place. Though the hideous conventions of overland writing, as he remarked to himself, surely needed improving upon. To that end, he had begun to keep a journal, which he was thinking of already as a book—the book it in fact later became: "The Western Attorney," by Elias Gray, Esq. It was one of the satisfactions known only to persons boasting a certain cultivation that the miseries of travel in primitive places among hinds who overreached themselves on every occasion, could be alleviated by the private comfort of trenchant observations upon strange sights, scrupulously set down in a rhetoric proudly in conformity with the best models. To salt the penetration of Lord Macaulay with the balance of Gibbon; the spirit of Dr. Johnson with the dispassion of Blackstone; while missing neither the flavor nor the outlandishness of Western sights: these, indeed, were ambitions worthy of the Missourian intellect which harbored them.

For would it not be a fitting chapter in the education of one who intended one day to make his mark in the halls of Clay and Calhoun, the rotundas of Webster and Polk, to observe coolly the perils and the savageries of life in the Western territories, and record them in prose of judgment and taste?

That the perils and savageries existed, he had no doubt. Testimonies were too frequently available on this point to be doubted.

Taos was the seat of an Indian capital. There had already been massacres and rebellions, slaughters and reprisals; and no end of parallel construction could be expended upon the exploits of a single creature, for example, Lieutenant Christopher Carson, of whom the chivalry of the entire nation had heard from boyhood on. No doubt there would be an occasion of propriety, at some assembly or ball or other polite function, in the course of which the young Western Attorney might reasonably expect to encounter, be presented to, and pass compliments upon, Colonel Carson himself, who still lived in Taos, though according to unkind rumor, with an Indian woman whom he had raised to the dignity of wife. Never mind. It behooved a cultivated mind to take into the wilderness not only the amenities of inherited grace but also an amused tolerance for whatever local prejudices had yet to yield to enlightenment.

Elias Gray was not yet thirty years of age, and had read every law book in the possession of United States Senator Thomas Hart Benton of Missouri. He was tall and slender, and had made a point of shaving every day during the crossing of the prairies along the Santa Fe Trail. His side-whiskers were of satiny gold, and there was high color in his cheeks. His eyes were a steady brown. He wore a curl above his pallid and serene brow. A resolution against unseemly mirth taken in his twelfth year had had its effect upon the cast of his countenance. He considered that a face always smiling betrayed a hollow geniality not to be found anywhere in Nature but in human simpletons, pity for whom could stop short of emulation.

Entering upon the vast plain approaching Taos in the late afternoon of that spring day in 1852, and resolving to keep calm in whatever contingency he might find himself, he, nevertheless, could not quite keep his heart from sinking at the prospect before him, when the driver of the army ambulance team, Sergeant Spiker, indicated the town of Taos. What he had agreeably taken for marks of distant erosion, a congeries of earthen mounds and squares huddled in the open light, was pronounced by the Sergeant to be the erections of the community.

Yet the stoutness of heart with which he had entered upon his mission did not abandon him now, and he remarked to the Sergeant that no doubt the official buildings were still lost to the view; the courtroom, for example, could hardly be contained in any one of these huts of clay, wattle, straw and scarcely finished, merely terminated, timber? The Sergeant was unable to say. He did say that court had sat here many a time, and would again; so doubtless there was some room large enough, and he wouldn't be *dis*-mayed to find that Estis's Tavern was the place, by day, that was.

Levity of this nature was not to be encouraged. Assistant United States Attorney Elias Gray watched in silence as the ambulance chinked and creaked through the barren streets, whose earthen sides simply turned up, stood on end, and became houses, with wooden doors and window frames.

Presently they reached what was no doubt called a plaza of sorts, a great square boxed on four sides by low buildings, very few of which had galleries or porches. Horses were tethered here and there. The twilight was oddly gentle over the scene, yet everything stood forth vividly. The Sergeant had orders to leave the Assistant United States Attorney to lodge with Captain Brewster, of the United States Cavalry, and did so, at one of the corner houses of the plaza. The Sergeant found nobody home, but let Elias Gray in and respectfully piled his two carpet bags, his Hamburg trunk of varnished raffia, his case of books, and his leather holster of guns and walking sticks, upon the bare floor of Captain Brewster's front room, and left to refresh his horses in the corral behind the plaza, and himself at the long table, or bar, of Estis's Tavern, where the first lights were showing deep in the wooden embrasures.

Elias stood in the door a moment.

Vivid and perilous! This heap of mud with scarcely a human ant crawling upon its mounds!

He laughed sarcastically and retired to an inner room where he found an army cot, and lay down for a rest. It was morning before he again saw where he was, and a party whom he took to be his host was rolled on the floor in an outlandish white and red woolen Indian rug, fast asleep, with his boots on and his hands peacefully folded upon an empty bottle. Humiliated at having usurped the Captain's bed, Elias arose and withdrew to his mound of luggage in the front room.

His silver watch told him he had best hasten to court, and he went out to the day, and was blinded by the sunlight. He crossed towards a small crowd before the Tavern. Not wholly unprepared, he heard that court was indeed in session within. Setting his jaw, he entered, made his way to the bench, presented his credentials in their oilskin wrappings to the Judge, and was instructed to sit down and wait until he was needed, while the murderer before the bar could be properly admonished and sentenced to hang.

All this was of course noted, later to be enshrined with appropriate irony and elegance in "The Western Attorney"; and so was the encounter with Captain Brewster, when at the end of seven days, the guest and the host managed to concatenate their activities and achieve a meeting; and so was the inspection of the Indian pueblo of Taos, which was barely dignified with the appellation of dwelling, and whose architecture was the despair of one committed to the refinements of the Greek taste; and so was the character of the Judge, who though he could read English was able to speak only Spanish, and with whom as a consequence justice was in constant peril of conforming to racial temperament instead of to universal principles; and so were the bleakness of the town, the savage prospect of mountain and desert upon which it looked, the stubbornness of the Indians in refusing to modify their tribal ways even after the administrative example of the United States was put before them; and, above all, there was noted, in that precise small handwriting, a certain evening when

Estis's was cleared for dancing and a man of parts might have been forgiven for expecting to have an opportunity to shine at last.

"Human society," he wrote, "of all Nature's instructive arrays of paradox and propriety, inclination and taste, affords to the dispassionate observer the widest varieties."

This observation was followed by an account of his last evening at Taos. Court had risen that day, and he was leaving upon the morrow for Santa Fe, in the train of the Judge and other functionaries of justice. The ball at Estis's was traditionally held to signalize the occasion. He wore his sky-blue coat and his fawn-colored trousers strapped underneath his boots, which had been made for him by Fichtlinger of St. Louis, and which pointed his toe for him very handsomely in the quadrille. He noticed early in the smoke-filled evening (even the women, the maidens, smoked, a detestable habit at best, but in their sex, reprehensible unutterably) how the bevy of girls in their shawls and voluminous skirts and powdered cheeks and stained lips giggled and flirted and whispered to each other about him, where he stood tall and fine-looking among the men on the opposite side of the narrow, long, low room where the lamps hung dim.

Nothing did warn him; nothing could have warned him. Sense could not possibly have conceived what suddenly occurred.

Two of the maidens, shrieking with laughter, charged across the creaky floor with their arms upraised, and he bowed to them gallantly. In one motion which not only accomplished their intention but swept them back across the room from him again, they brought their hands down upon his orderly curls and smashed whole eggshells filled with cologne water upon his head. The liquid stank and stung him in the eyes, and ran down upon his padded coat and his velvet waistcoat with the white forget-me-nots embroidered upon it. The room roared with fun and approval. The musicians made up rhymes about him in Spanish. The men slapped him on the back. A youth brought him two eggshells similarly prepared, and urged him across the floor to smash them upon the heads of the expectant young ladies. In a daze he found himself doing this. Quite evidently a local convention had been observed in triumph. He then engaged speechlessly in a dance with one of his oddly acquired admirers. The plaster walls rang and rang with merriment and music. At the end of the dance, he stood panting in a corner, when a small, elderly seeming individual cleared his throat delicately and spoke to him, putting out a wrinkled and modest hand with diffidence from the engulfing cuff of a coat too big for him.

"My name's Carson!" he said, and smiled rather like a crabapple, in the face, and then having made this gesture of friendliness to a stranger, turned and shuffled away, as if having accomplished his one possible social task for the evening.

Elias spoke magnificently to him, in a rather Bentonian fashion, the democratic grandeur of the congressional style, and too late realized that he had been accosted by the famous hero of the plains and the mountains, who had gone home to his small house up the street with the raw-wood gallery out front.

The dancers moved to a guitar and a flute made of wood.

All night the music went on; or possibly he dreamed of it long later.

He slept wretchedly. In vain he sought to compose his thoughts. They were almost like the thoughts of fever, cigarette smoke from pretty mouths, a little old hand plucking cordially at him out of a history of unimaginable valor, a cascade of perfume across his eyes, the heavy army wagon crawling up a cliff road in the mountains, the curious unawareness of the citizens of Taos that they were outlandish in every possible way.

Barely had he composed his mind and fallen asleep, when it seemed time to get up and set out again on his travels. Later, the pages of his composition served him in a new capacity; gave him haven, let him be sure again of things, in restful echoes of Lord Macaulay's temper and Mr. Gibbon's manner.

IV ———— 1893

THE RIVAL PROPHETS

H E'D HARDLY BEEN in Taos an hour when he made arrangements to hire by the day the buckboard which had brought him from the D. & R.G. station over at Embudo. He explained that on some days he might not want it at all; on others he might be out from dawn to dark; did not want to have to bother to see if the buckboard and team were free, simply wanted to order them to come around for him at the Columbian Hotel on the plaza, where he could step in and be off on his investigating. Investigating was the word quoted to everyone by Luke Martin, who owned the buckboard and met the train twice a week at Embudo. Luke said the gentleman gave his card to him, fetched it out of the lower right-hand pocket of his brocaded vest, handed it over, waved at the younger man with him and said, "This's my secretary, Captain Rory, be glad to have you act on his orders," and entered into the Columbian leaving a long drawn out sort of *cloud* of cigar smoke behind him. The card said B. W. Cornelius, in the middle, and then down on the left side, sort of, smaller, but still, elegant and clear, though slopy and having fancy tails on the letters, *Creative Industrialist*. What in the hell it meant, Luke did not know.

However, the next day the truth was less elegantly out. Mr. Cornelius was a promoter. He called at the bank, and at the office of the newspaper, and received visitors in the lobby at the Columbian, and by nightfall, there was legend abroad. Many a local resident fell asleep that night a far richer man, if plans could do it. It was as if Mr. Cornelius had awakened them. Here they'd been living here, and *living here*, and seeing nothing of what lay right under their noses. Why, man, immense! he said, the possibilities are simply immense! And he talked and talked, and his voice got richer and huskier, and they ordered whisky around, and cigars, here, Captain Rory, take my little brass key, here, and go down the hall to my room, and fetch out that tin of cigars in my leather box. He was a heavy man, sitting like a cinnamon bear in the lobby of the Columbian, moving his massive paws in slow, rich gestures, and occasionally stroking his brocaded front in a sign of well-being. He never smiled. He hung his heavy head forward and spoke slowly and with a hint of Texas drawl at the fascinated citizen he was converting, and he wagged his head slowly to emphasize his dream and his small blue eyes watered a little at the beauty, the energy, of what possessed him.

They now understood his visiting card, and each one of them had a copy of it folded into his wallet, and could take it out and muse alone, later, on the phrase *Creative Industrialist*, and go off into lonely admiration of the forces of the grand world, concentrated and made purposeful in such a man as B. W. Cornelius.

He explained that his private car was on the siding at Maxwell City, on the tracks of the Santa Fe, that was. He'd made a grand loop, gone up to Colorado, picked up the Denver & Rio Grande there, and come down the valley to the junction of Embudo. Never had he seen such land. What were they all thinking of? Did they not know fortune when it arose from the God's earth and smote them between the eyes?

He dared to be almost wrathful, and they hung their heads. And then he relaxed and his voice grew grave and gentle, and he said that if they would give him a few days to look around with Captain Rory, his secretary and consulting engineer, one and the same, he would be able to sketch his ideas a little more specifically the next time they talked.

He arose in the lobby of the Columbian, ending an audience. He stood and shook hands with all the local gentlemen, sending them off with a slight dismissive pressure in the direction of the door, murmuring "Millions! Millions, if ever I saw"; and at last they were gone, and the immemorially remote and silent plain, the mountain behind the pueblo, the stillest sunlight in memory, seemed qualities of another and more innocent country.

He used Martin's buckboard for days, and his agility, for one so stout, amazed everyone. He was approached slyly by various individuals when he was known to've returned to the hotel for the night; each asking for a special ear; a hint; a cute chance, just a trifle ahead of— But he resisted them all soberly, saying, "Not yet, not yet. I am studying on it. Studying on it. Good evening, sir, if you will," and they left him ablaze with joy over his integrity, his immovability.

The day after he came back from a trip to Elizabethtown to see the new mines opening up there, one, and two, and three man ventures, he was observed to be sitting for hours, brooding in the lobby. No one dared approach him except Captain Rory, who kept bringing him papers which he signed without glancing at them. Captain Rory tiptoed, a slender, mustached young man with the tragic distinction of a drunkard's eye, roving in wistful geniality the faces of all whom he could see. B. W. Cornelius was believed to be deeply pensive over something. The one or two citizens who did venture to address him got looked at so absently, so unseeingly, that they could not take offense at receiving no answer; they knew, they *said* they knew, that he was just simply a-*way* off, some'eres, a-workin' and a-creatin' and didn't even know they'd spoke to him. A local ironist announced at the bar of the saloon around noon that ol' B.W. was sittin' over in the Columbian, thinkin', and it was a sight to see, and all afternoon men dawdled past, and looked in, and sure enough, he was still sitting there, like a bear expecting winter.

There were only a handful, three or four, who were not impressed. They were recent citizens, friendly but addled fellows, who said they came to Taos "to paint." There was a brief period of confusion as to what this meant until it turned out that they meant to paint pictures, by hand, on canvas, with tubes of color, etc. They had been seen out of doors, staring at the Indian pueblo, or making an Indian stand there in the sunshine with his blanket on, or an Indian woman with a black pot on her head; and painting them. They were ardent young men, bearded, voluble, sighting everything they saw over their thumbs, and later poking their thumbs in the air to describe to others that which had enchanted them. To make pictures of *around here?* thought the local residents, shaking their heads, and coming to mind of what everybody knew, so commonly, that desert plain, that harsh mountain, that set of mud blocks where those peculiarly remote Indians lived, what was there to exclaim over in an Indian jar, or a striped blanket, or bright sunshine on a 'dobe wall? But the bearded young fellows laughed and shrugged and went on making pictures, certain of the riches they had found.

The thing was, they just couldn't be moved by the kind of riches B. W. Cornelius was after. They said, freely, that they hoped he would accidentally poke a hole in his stomach, and just fade away like a punctured balloon, and then Taos would be safe again.

Safe?

Certainly, they explained, the quickest way to ruin this paradise for artists and sensitive people and thinkers of all kinds would be to commercialize it.

Such words stirred anger up in those who heard them.

If B.W. hadn't come suddenly and majestically out of his hibernation, there might've been trouble. He clapped his hands, as it were, and summoned the local capitalists, the men of vision, as he called them, and gave them the fruits of his meditations and discoveries.

He received them in the hotel lobby.

He said he *saw* the whole thing now.

He gathered their eyes by roving their faces with his small blue eyes. Each heart knew a pang, as when touched by prophecy. He began to speak through cigar smoke, the blue tail of smoke drifting past his ponderous brow as if in sacrifice. He said people needed to come into the valley. This meant railroads. He had the answer. A hasty survey showed the thorough practicability of a direct railroad connection to be built into Taos from Maxwell City—the A.T. & S.F. right of way over there (where his private car was waiting for him on a siding). He said the land would doubtless be populated with marvellous rapidity following such a construction.

Not only to bring people in, he said, but to take products out.

[61]

The mines at E-town, for instance, he said, shagging his great head at them soberly, on the eastern side of the range, and the rich mineral districts of Rio Hondo, Copper Mountain, Picuris and Arroyo Hondo on the western side, all should be fed and drained by an extension of another rail connection, the Union Pacific spur from Trinidad, Colorado, to Vásquez, in Colfax County.

"With the building of this road," he stated, "a sudden change will come over this valley."

He made the change, in the air, with his suddenly lofted paw, holding it there while he gazed at them. His words took their breath away.

"Moreover": if they wanted profound, basic, practical proof that he knew what he was talking about, the Maxwell City spur survey indicated that the roadbed would be seventy-three and a half miles long, have a maximum curvature of eight degrees, and a grade not to exceed two per cent. He cleared his throat in a growl and paused.

Fascinated silence.

"Now what have you?" he demanded, and answered them. They had 25,000 to 30,000 acres under cultivation now, by 10,000 people, in a-l-l the valley. With intensive cultivation, there could be 50,000 population, allowing a ten-acre fruit farm to each family of five persons. One orchard of five acres would yield $400 an acre; ten acres intensely cultivated would thus yield $4,000.

Magnificent?

Magnificent.

"But," he said, blowing gusty breaths of authority and smoke, "there is a major flaw in this prospect, for there is no water for irrigation on such a scale, on the western slope of the range."

He let them be rueful for just long enough.

"Yet if there is a major flaw, there is also a major solution."
What was it?

A canal, a mammoth canal, to be dug from a point near Conejos, Colorado, on the Rio Grande, to water these lands. It would irrigate 100,000 acres, and the trees would rise and the fruits would drop, and the grains of the temperate zone would flourish.

"Apples," he pronounced, with stinging relish that made their mouths water, "apricots, pears, peaches, plums, nectarines. Potatoes, beets, turnips, parsnips, onions, celery. Alfalfa."

All these were already grown there; but he made their scale sound prodigious, and they discovered the excellence of these products as if for the first time.

Someone asked what the canal would cost.

"Millions," Mr. Cornelius replied, with the small lids of his eyes dropped half across his vision. "We shall naturally have to think in millions."

He went on to the mineral prospects; said that he had specimens of gold assayed at $20,000 to the ton. West of Tres Piedras he personally had found veins of ferruginous ore with the mica beds. Why send $25,000,000 annually to England for tin, when west of Tres Piedras tin was abundant?

The scale was staggering. How could they resist him? What did they have to do?

They didn't have to do anything, yet. He was just making a preliminary survey, in fact, would confess that he was interested in looking over a good many other locations in the West. He would now return "East" to his boards of directors, and make reports on what he had seen. The local banker, the newspaper man, the two leading merchants had private audiences with him later, and their faces were full of pleading. To encourage them, he uttered the names of Eastern capitalists whom he might undertake to interest in the valley when the time seemed ripe—Carnegie, Hill, Frick, Doremus, Summerdown—

The West was full of prophets who brought the new industrial hope, dazzled whole populations with golden statistics, and after obeying the laws of the prophet's nature, vanished into legend and left behind them only the local reality which seemed bitter, for a time, because it was so familiar, and needed forgiving so many days of a man's life . . .

Mr. B. W. Cornelius caught the up-valley train over at Embudo the next morning.

The great canal was never dug. No railroad ever reached Taos. The mines of E-town petered out and closed down. The spur from Maxwell City remained only a survey, beautiful with its eight degree maximum curvature and two percent grade. Eventually the D. & R.G. itself abandoned the line through Embudo, 28 miles away. The desert, the blue range, the lazy little ditches were unchanged by the industrial dreams of the Nineties, and the realities of the new century.

The clever, ardent, bearded young men went on painting pictures. If change was destined to come, they were its prophets.

V ——— 1923

SO LITTLE FREEDOM

ONE MORNING, after he had been in Taos about a week, young Roger Warrington went into the Plaza Drug Store for a chocolate soda at about half past ten. Just being in Taos, New Mexico, was almost enough, he had thought; but his astonishment and delight were almost like being a little sick when he saw, reflected in the soda fountain mirror, the two rather large women come in, followed by the small, spring-footed man with the fiery red beard. Roger could hardly believe his eyes. The three people sat down noisily at one of the drugstore tables, ordered soft drinks, and sat regarding each other. There was quite a crowd in the Plaza Drug; nobody paid them any mind but Roger; but his heart was beating fast, and he felt almost weak, because it was unmistakably his favorite novelist, Edward St David, especially now that he had pulled off his ten-gallon hat, and the thick hair fell fox-red over his incandescent white brow. The soda jerker took them their drinks, and one of the women said in a comfortable voice, unconsciously loud so everyone could hear, but in a German accent,

"*Ja!* the chocolate szoda is yours, St David; it will give you cr-r-amps again."

This must be his Austrian wife, Roger had read about their romance, and he gazed at her and felt somehow comfortable about her. St David screwed up his eyes and merely stared at her, and took the straw into his mouth like a greedy child.

The other woman was impassive; she seemed almost like a governess for the two of them. Roger suddenly knew who she was; it was that rich woman from Boston who had built a medieval castle of adobe out near the pueblo, with a high wall where at night the lanterns shone deep in the roadway leading to the door; and now everybody came to Taos to visit her, from anywhere, famous writers and painters and publishers and symphony conductors; her name was Mrs. Gerald Boree. Most everybody in Taos was always saying her name, "Mrs Boree, M'ss B'ree," a sort of refrain of curious respect, except that the young painters who idled in the plaza spoke of her with comic intention and effect simply as "Bertha." She had left her husband, Gerald Boree the artist, in Rapallo, and had come here alone "to find herself," as she had so often tried to do.

St David sucked air at the bottom of his soda glass, and began to speak to Mrs. Boree, who appeared to be enacting the conception of placidity.

"A new kind of manorial bad manners," he sneered. "My ancestors used to have to put up with getting beaten and robbed and starved and bastardized by the manor folk, who carried on like this in full view of the county, elevated above common decency and poor trouble, as if just and right. This is a new dimension of the same thing. Moving in and taking over a whole town, a damned whole contented and centuries-old secure people, and putting them on like a new rag to wear around your shoulders, to show to the rich and famous and talented and frightful people you drag here from all over the world to see your show, your personal mountains, your private desert, the spiritual reservoir which you did not fill, but only saw others filling and taking from."

In embarrassment Roger lowered his eyes from the big soda fountain mirror where he had seen all. The drugstore was full of the midmorning glisten and drift of casual life. Everybody could hear. Roger was blushing; his ears were like red lampshades, he knew, with light coming through them. When he dared look again, he was astonished to see the group at the round iron table sitting in simple composure. Mrs. Boree was gazing at the great man without resentment, almost with love? do you think? and her face was like a daytime moon under her black hair with its Pueblo bangs. Mrs. St David looked almost bored, a bored lioness, sleepily licking the sweet edge of her chocolate glass. St David himself was hunched bonily down, sucking on the straw, scowling. And even then, he looked up, and smiled sort of washily, his resentment free, his blue eyes striking out with a look of misery and power which gave Roger a pang in the breast. But the shrill, bitten voice was not yet able to be quiet.

"And do not sit there understanding me with possessive tolerance," he said. "I won't have it. Whatever I owed you I have paid you. I came, did I not? You have exhibited me, have you not? We have had our thrust and parry; I like your damned insolent landscape, and I shall flee it the moment I can afford to, and you shall have suitable credit for discovering my inner appropriateness with it."

"St David!" said his wife, richly chiding in her Viennese accent, "I beleef it is your manners which are too bad. You are too *bad*, to sit here in vront of all these beoble, and show your temper like a stomach-ache."

"Ha!" he cried, turning on her, "if there is one thing worse than to be mooned over, it is to be shut off, like a doll! I know you! Mocking me with your big female calm, waiting . . ."

"Come, Bertha," said Gerda St David rising. "He is going to be dreadful all day."

Roger saw the three of them leave the drugstore, St David in the rear of the two large women, his new blue jeans sticking stiffly out behind where his bony hams failed to fill them, his head dwarfed like a rabbit's by the tall, ear-like rise of his ten-gallon hat, his rough woolen lumberjack shirt, bright red plaid, bagging pitifully around his thin shoulders and arms with a sort of childish pretension and failure. St David coughed as he disappeared into the blazing sunshine of the sidewalk crowd. His cough shook him throughout his whole skeleton. Roger Warrington swallowed in sympathy. Then even genius was not free? Could look ridiculous? Was tortured and had to cry out, over even the silliest things?

No matter. Roger's youthful loyalty was truer than that. He had actually set eyes on Edward St David, and if he accomplished no other thing, his trip to Taos that summer was already worthwhile.

But his hungers, too, were truer, harder to satisfy than by such a glimpse. He went out to the country where Mrs. Boree's house was, and sure enough something happened. Mrs. St David came walking out alone, toward the dirt highway, and before he knew it, they were talking together, and he never felt so easy with anybody in his life. She had him saying in two minutes that her husband was his idol, and it didn't make her laugh, or be modest, or anything; she simply said he must come back with her to the house and meet him. Her warmth, her allowance of him, right off, made Roger a little blurred with joy; after all, look who she was, a former countess, and the wife of the greatest living writer, and she said she thought she had seen Roger before, at the drugstore? drinking a szo-da? *Ja?*

He was too scared to go with her to meet St David. But he wrung her hand, and she smiled broadly, said she had two sons of her own, and hoped he was a happy boy, "—are you content, here, in Ta-os?" She didn't wait for him to reply, but went on to say that he must not break his heart if he didn't have any tal-ent, but go home, and be happy with the good, and dear, kind things at home; sometimes they were hard to find, but *ja!* they existed, everywhere. She blinked both her light blue eyes at him, and went back up the long road to the house of which so many mysteries were reported in the village, and left him staring after her, startled and moved.

No talent? . . . It had never occurred to him.

That would mean they were right, the others, who were ashamed of him, back home in Whitewater, Texas, and of the love he had in him and could not conceal, but had to reveal as art. Yet how kindly, how immediately, Mrs. St David seemed to know him.

He didn't know which one he loved more, St David or his wife. Roger had the disturbing and exciting belief that anything could happen in Taos. Drifting up and down the dried mud streets, he conceived of himself as living the most adventurous life possible. It took so little freedom in the realm of the possible to make him happy. He was blond-headed, as they say in Texas, pink-cheeked, and slow moving. He longed to think and feel and believe as independently as his grandfather had pioneered and killed and colonized.

But when he got back to his room by the alfalfa field, he found a letter from his mother, Texas-Anne. It was an edict. Big Roger said if he did not take the next bus out of Taos, they would never send him any more money, and they were going to settle once and for all about this thing. And Grandfather had deeded his stock in the Bank to Little Roger, and if he came right home, and went to work in the Bank, and learned the business, they'd put him on the Board of Directors on his twenty-first birthday. So wouldn't he do this, hon? just for her? She missed her little baby boy, and was sure he couldn't bear to refuse Texas-Anne the only thing she ever asked of him?

His exultation vanished. He bitterly thought of how both Mrs. St David and his mother had in effect asked him to do the same thing. How could they both be right about him? He dawdled for several days, not even answering the letter. He still had enough money for a while, even if they never gave him another cent. He said to himself that he was too upset to paint. He found himself hanging around in front of Mrs. Boree's gateway; or out in the fields beyond her house; or down in an arroyo from which everything was out of sight but the tip of the blue mountain. Approaching the place, one afternoon, he heard St David talking, and he could not go away. In a moment he saw St David, and that he was talking to a large sandy-looking cow.

"Life uncritical; life absolute; life abstract," he was saying, almost in song. "You ruminate and gestate and let your generous bag to anyone who desires it. Oh purity of unthought! Heavenly vacuity!"

But he knew whenever anyone was looking, and he turned swiftly on Roger, and slitted his blue-eyed glance suspiciously. Roger stammered something, and started away, but St David began to laugh, a high delighted laugh.

"The drugstore baby!" he cried. "Gerda told me you came to call the other day and then dwindled off in a storm of nerves. . . . I wouldn't bite you. . . . I have been having the sweetest of all arguments with my cow here, a one-sided argument. Come here!"

St David took his hand.

"Why is your hand cold?"

Roger explained that—that he was excited, meeting this way after years of admiring him from afar.

"Rot."

St David sat down on a clump of salt grass and waved Roger before him. In a twinkling, Roger was pouring out his troubles, and St David was nodding, as if ahead of him in the tale. His eyes smoldered and began to fire. His spirit always burned at the news of cruelty, of anyone's hope being maimed; and he interrupted Roger by jumping up and walking away and coming back.

"Never, never, never, *never* give in!" he almost shrieked. It took all his strength, and he began to cough. He hugged his wracking ribs and bent over, and the coughs travelled up from the ground and shook him as if he were a fiery red cat in the grasp of a huge dog. Roger was alarmed, but St David managed to wave off his concern. In a little while the seizure was over, and in the sunlit silence they met each other with little smiles. In that recuperative quiet another voice then sounded. It came from the rim of the arroyo above them. It said, coolly, musically,

"Well if you need proof there it is, Edward. If you will waste yourself on everything else but the one thing that matters, which is your work, which I could protect for you—"

It was Bertha Morgan Boree, looking down upon them impassively. But her eyes had lights of ire in them, and she looked from the boy to the man and back again. Roger thought she even looked jealous, but he at once said to himself *that* was a crazy idea.

St David seemed for a moment too outraged to speak. When at last he could speak he was so controlled that he was more terrifying than he was in his outbursts.

"You have been watching me in secret," he said. His voice was thin with contained rage. "When will I ever learn to believe my wife! Nobody could have seen me come here otherwise. It is all I needed to know.—Come along, you, lad, we will finish talking in the fields, in broad view of a purer heaven."

He turned and scrambled up the opposite slope of the arroyo with costly energy. The dirt flew down under his hands and feet. Roger clambered after him, astonished at the power within that delicate frame.

"Edward! Oh, *do* be sensible and careful," called Mrs. Boree, raising her voice but still sounding most cultivated. "How you misunderstand me! I only feel a duty—"

On the opposite edge of the red arroyo he turned and made an obscene gesture at her across the gap, and then fled to the fields, walking loosely and with incredible speed. Words trailed back over his working shoulders to Roger, angry words, foul, execratory. At last, a long way across the field, they stopped, and turned, and looked. The bulky figure of the woman was still at the arroyo. Her hands were to the sky. She was posed like a priestess. Roger was impressed. Feeling that, St David said to him,

"She knew we would turn to look."

They walked on in silence for a quarter of an hour, and the calm of the day, the desert scent, wry and pungent, the peace of the looming mountain, the gold of the wheat in the fields before the pueblo, which was darker gold in the sunshine, came back into them, and St David finally said to the boy,

"Well, *I* never, never, never, never gave in, and I never

shall! *I would rather be killed by what I am than by what somebody else wants me to be."*

His eyes in the white face, under the dark red bang, raked and swept Roger with a sort of rough compassionate tenderness. He seized the boy's hand and crushed it in his, and then he nodded, saying "Goodbye, goodbye, we know each other now, those things keep. Goodbye!" He turned and walked away in a solitude which defied further intrusion.

That night Roger slept out on the roof of the adobe house where he was living. It was a sort of ritual, under the stars of Taos, farewell, made of joy and grief both. One thing he was sure of. It took a "genius" to say that about *never, never, never, never*: and he vaguely felt that he had been *through* something, but he wasn't quite clear about what it was. He lay awake a long time, thinking of everything he had seen and done in Taos, where he loved the busy, commercial, gregarious to-do about "art."

But he knew, too, after those brief but somehow total glimpses of the St Davids, yes, and of Mrs. Boree, that there were trials he had never suspected about art in the souls where it lived, and required delivery. He fell asleep at peace, knowing that he carried no fires within him such as were consuming Edward St David; and the next day he went back to Whitewater, Texas, and the Bank.